A COUNTRY ON THE MOVE

The United States from 1900 – 1929

by Mary C. Turck

Perfection Learning®

Cover and book design: Michelle J. Glass

About the Author

Mary Turck is a freelance writer who lives in Minnesota with her husband, Ron Salzberger, and their two daughters, Molly and Macy. In addition to being an author, Mary has also worked as a teacher and a lawyer.

Image Credits: Denver Public Library, Western History Collection pp. 6 (upper-left & lower right), 8 (left), 38, 40, 57, 61; Records of the Redpath Chautauqua Collection, Special Collections Department, University of Iowa Libraries, Iowa City, Iowa p. 9 (left); ©Bettmann/CORBIS pp. 19, 29 (left), 34, 42 (left); ©Underwood & Underwood/CORBIS p. 29 (right)

ArtToday (some images copyright www.arttoday.com) cover, pp. 5, 6, (bottom-left), 8 (right), 9 (right), 10, 11, 13, 14, 18, 23, 36, 37, 43, 44, 50, 51, 53, 55, 60, 62, 63, 66; Library of Congress pp. 7, 15, 20, 21, 25, 28, 39, 42 (right), 46, 54, 62; ©CORBIS royalty-free p. 33

Perfection Learning® Corporation, 1000 North Second Avenue,
P.O. Box 500, Logan, Iowa 51546-0500.
Phone: 1-800-831-4190 • Fax: 1-800-543-2745
perfectionlearning.com
Paperback ISBN 0-7891-5548-6
Cover Craft® ISBN 0-7569-0635-0
Printed in the U.S.A.

Table *of* Contents

THE AMERICAN CENTURY?

$\mathcal{A}$ new century dawned. The United States was flexing its muscles. The country was free, united, and strong. It was ready to claim greatness.

Its population was growing. Its industries led the world.

The United States had just won the Spanish-American war with Spain. Now the country led an empire. It ruled the Philippines. It **dominated** Cuba and Latin America. This would be the American century!

Spanish-American War

Cuba was fighting for independence from Spain. The United States supported Cuba by sending the battleship *Maine* to Cuba. It was to turn back Spanish ships trying to enter Cuba's harbors.

The United States entered into war with Spain in April of 1898 after the Spanish sunk the *Maine*. In August 1898, the United States and Spain ended the war and signed a treaty. The treaty gave Cuba its freedom. The United States controlled the tiny country until it was fully independent in 1901. The treaty also gave the United States possession of Puerto Rico and Guam and control of the Phillipines.

Of course, not everyone agreed.

Even the empire had **critics**. They did not think the United States should rule Cuba or the Philippines. They didn't want the United States to tell Latin Americans what to do. They did not want their country to be a **bully**.

For millions, the century began in bitter poverty. However, a few people were very rich. Two percent of the people owned sixty percent of the country's wealth. Just 44 families earned more than a million dollars per year.

Many people were poor. Most workers earned $500 per year. Others earned less.

The new century held no promise for people of color. Most African Americans lived in poverty. Slavery had ended with the Civil War.

Now debt and fear created a new form of slavery. White landowners used debt to keep blacks down. Terror and **lynchings** threatened their lives.

Native Americans had been driven from their land. They were forced onto **reservations**. And over time, much of this reservation land was taken from them. Until 1924, Native Americans were not even considered citizens.

The United States was growing fast. Much of this growth came from **immigration**.

Many citizens were afraid of immigrants. They especially feared the "new immigrants." They came from places like Poland, Italy, and China. They seemed different from the English and Germans, who had come first.

⌁ PROGRESSIVE PRESIDENTS ⌁

In 1900, William McKinley was elected to his second term as president.

McKinley

He easily won the election. Teddy Roosevelt was his vice president. In 1901, McKinley was **assassinated**. Roosevelt charged onto center stage, and he instantly charmed the country.

Roosevelt

6

Rough Riders

Roosevelt was already a national hero. He had fought in the Spanish-American War in 1898. He led a volunteer **cavalry** unit called the Rough Riders. People remembered the Rough Riders' famous battles. Many credited Roosevelt for winning the war.

Roosevelt was a Republican and a Progressive. The Progressive movement included Democrats and Republicans. Progressives thought government should be efficient. They wanted to end **corruption** and limit the power of large corporations. They felt people should participate in government, and government should help people.

Taft

Large corporations had lots of power. They joined together in **trusts**. They agreed not to compete with one another. Instead, they cooperated and kept prices high.

Progressives wanted to break up trusts. They wanted to end price-fixing. Roosevelt was called a *trustbuster*. He talked about breaking up trusts.

But Roosevelt did not succeed. His political action failed to place many limits on big business and big money.

William Howard Taft became president in 1909 after Roosevelt. Roosevelt had decided not to run again. Taft was another Republican and a Progressive. But his presidency disappointed many Progressives.

In 1912, Teddy Roosevelt changed his mind and ran against Taft. But the Republicans would not nominate Roosevelt. So he formed his own party.

A reporter asked Roosevelt how he felt. He replied "Strong as a bull moose!" From then on, his party was called the Bull Moose Progressives.

The Republican voters split. Some voted for Taft. Others voted for Roosevelt. Because of the split, Woodrow Wilson, a Democrat, became president.

Wilson

President Wilson tried to limit the power of big money interests. Like the others, he was unsuccessful.

All three presidents, Roosevelt, Taft, and Wilson, were Progressives. They all talked about helping the little people. They all fell short of Progressive ideals.

Sometimes it seemed that the U.S. government was run by big business. Government seemed to have less power than business.

⤐ THIRD PARTIES ⤕

LaFollette

In 1924, Robert LaFollette ran for president. He was a Republican senator and a Progressive. He ran for president as a Progressive and received 13 percent of the vote.

During this time, the **Socialist** Party won many followers. Socialists supported women's rights. They worked for **unions**.

In Oklahoma, Socialists were very popular. More than a hundred Socialists won political office in 1914.

Eugene Debs ran as the Socialist candidate for president in 1908. He received 420,793 votes. That was 2.8 percent of the total. In 1912, he ran again. This time he received 900,000 votes.

Debs

The biggest changes of the century did not come from government. They did not come from business. They came from ordinary people.

Millions of immigrants helped America grow. They came to the U.S. on their own. They built their own communities. They brought their own cultures. The immigrants changed and enriched American culture.

Where presidents failed, workers succeeded. They curbed the power of big business. They organized unions.

The unions forced changes. They forced businesses to sign contracts. They persuaded politicians to change laws. Unions protected workers.

Women joined together in a movement for **suffrage**. They marched, wrote, begged, and spoke. Finally, they won the right to vote.

Other people joined the Prohibition movement. They wanted to ban drinking. They succeeded in banning alcohol in the United States.

10

But other people rebelled. They wanted to make their own choices about drinking alcohol. They, too, organized. They fought to **repeal** Prohibition. They eventually succeeded.

Throughout these exciting years, great changes happened.

⟶ THE AMERICAN DREAM ⟵

In Massachusetts, women worked 13 hours a day. They spun cotton into thread. Bone-tired, they dreamed. They dreamed of six-day workweeks and eight-hour workdays. They dreamed of better schools for their children.

In Colorado, miners burrowed deep into the ground. They worked, shut away from the sun. They dreamed of a brighter tomorrow.

In Alabama, the children of slaves bent their backs in cotton fields. They knew that freedom should not look like this. But they kept the dream of freedom alive.

In Minnesota, farmers planted wheat and corn. They waited for rain and sun. They prayed for good harvests. They buried children, dead from **diphtheria, influenza,** and **scarlet fever.** They dreamed of enough money to pay the **mortgage** and keep the farm.

In Ireland, Poland, Italy, and China, men and women dreamed. "America" was the name of their dream. They saved and boarded ships for America. That bright dream shone before them.

The American dream promised freedom and security to immigrants. It promised enough to eat and a roof over their heads. It promised schools for children and a better life for those who worked hard.

By the millions, people dreamed the American dream. Often, those who shared the dream worked together. As they joined together, they changed the face of America.

chapter 2

IMMIGRATION—
RESHAPING A COUNTRY

People sailed across the oceans, drawn by hope. Almost 500,000 new people arrived in 1900. More than 600,000 came in 1902. In 1905, more than 1 million arrived. Even more followed in 1906 and 1907.

The men usually arrived first. They were packed in ships like sardines. They came looking for work. And they found it! The immigrants farmed on the Great Plains. They worked in factories. They built railroads.

⟜═ ONE FAMILY AMONG MANY ═⟜

Sonya Kevar lived in Russia as a child. Her father came to America in 1906. He sent back money to feed his family. He wrote letters telling them of life in America.

For five years, Sonya's father **scrimped** and saved. Finally, he had enough money for tickets for his family.

By now, Sonya was 13. She and her mother, brothers, and sisters prepared to go to America.

First, they rode in a horse-drawn wagon, This took them to a bigger town. Then they traveled on a train. The train took them to a port city. Finally, they boarded a ship for America.

The family had bought the cheapest tickets. On the ship, they lived on the bottom deck. The ship was crowded. Many people were seasick.

After 21 days, the ship arrived in America. The Kevars were five people among the 878,587 immigrants coming to America in 1911.

⟜═ LIFE IN THE BIG CITY ═⟜

Most immigrants first arrived in New York City. Their ships stopped at Ellis Island. This was the processing center for immigrants. Many of them settled in New York.

In the city, immigrants crowded into **tenements**. A typical tenement stood four or five stories tall. Each floor had four apartments. Each apartment had a front room, a kitchen, and a small bedroom.

Parents, children, and perhaps a grandparent shared the small apartment. A kitchen fireplace or stove burned wood or coal. This provided a cooking fire and heated the apartment.

Water came from a pump outside. Like groceries, water had to be carried up the wooden stairs to the apartment. Garbage was placed in a box in front of the building. Bathrooms were privies in the backyard.

A privy is also called an *outhouse*. It is an outdoor toilet. A privy has a door and a seat with a hole in it. Sometimes a privy sits above a pit. Sometimes it empties into a sewer.

Abraham Beame came to New York in 1906. He was just a baby then. He remembered his early years in *Ellis Island Interviews: In Their Own Words* by Peter Morton Coan.

> *We all lived in tenements. They were known as railroad flats. You had a living room, a kitchen, and one or two bedrooms. I remember we used to sleep three to a bed. I slept with my two brothers. The tenements were heated by coal. But you had to buy your own coal and your own ice to put in the **icebox**. Vendors would come around and we would buy from them. The apartments were lit by gaslight. The toilet was down the hall. You shared them [sic] with the other apartments. I remember one place I lived where the toilet was an outhouse in the yard.*

When Abraham Beame grew up, he became a politician. In 1973, he was elected mayor of New York City.

⊹═ MOVING ON ═⊹

For many people, New York was just the first stop. Some people moved on to the coal mines of Pennsylvania. Others settled in Chicago, Milwaukee, or Duluth. Many rolled cigars in Florida. Some tended grapevines in California or plowed the prairies in Minnesota. Still others built the railroads that connected the entire nation.

CHINESE IMMIGRANTS

Immigrants arrived on the west coast too. The first Chinese immigrants came before 1850. They settled in San Francisco. Many had been fishermen in China. So they worked in the fishing industry. Others mined gold. Many worked to build the railroads.

Chinese immigrants were victims of **racism**. One law said Chinese immigrants couldn't become citizens. Another said they could not buy farmland. Another prevented them from owning gold mines.

In 1882, Congress passed another anti-Chinese law. This one said Chinese men could not bring their wives to America.

As new laws took away opportunities, the Chinese immigrants changed. When they could not own land, they rented it. They raised vegetables and fruits. Then they sold produce door-to-door. Some became **migrant** farmworkers. Others became merchants or ran laundries. Many worked in construction.

Prejudice sometimes turned to violence. Lee Chew was an early immigrant. He first worked as a servant to an American family. Then he opened a laundry. He worked from 7 a.m. to midnight, five days a week. He saved his money. He endured much racism and some mob violence. According to Lee Chew, more than half of the Chinese in America wanted to become citizens. "But how can they make this country their home as [the laws] are now?" he asked.

Some newcomers did not come from foreign countries. They moved from one part of the United States to another. Millions of people moved from farms to cities. Many of these people were African Americans leaving the South.

In the South, African Americans could see no future. They lived as **sharecroppers** or **tenant** farmers on someone else's land. Each year, sharecroppers paid the landowners a share of their crop as rent. Tenants paid cash rent.

The landowners also owned the supply stores. The farmers bought seed, food, and clothes from these stores. The landowners kept the books. At harvesttime, they figured what the farmers owed. Sometimes the farmers had a few dollars left over. Often, they just ended up deeper in debt.

The South held other troubles for blacks. Jim Crow laws kept blacks and whites strictly **segregated**. Whites had better schools, jobs, and homes. Blacks had what was left. A black man was called *boy*. A white man was called *sir*. African Americans who protested put their lives at risk.

Jim Crow laws were passed by many Southern states in the late 1800s. They stated that African Americans and whites were to use separate public facilities. This included restrooms, railroad cars, telephone booths, gambling tables, and even Bibles for swearing in witnesses.

Several Supreme Court decisions in the 1950s and 1960s and the Civil Rights Act of 1964 made most of these laws **invalid.**

During the 1920s, the Ku Klux Klan grew stronger. The Klan targeted African Americans, Catholics, Jews, and foreigners.

By 1924, the Klan claimed to have four or five million members. The KKK burned crosses in front of people's homes. It terrorized black men and women. Between 1918 and 1927, about 450 people were lynched in the United States. Of those, 416 were African American.

The Ku Klux Klan was formed by a group of Confederate Army veterans in Tennessee around 1865. The Klan believed in the superiority of whites over African Americans. Members often used violence to achieve their goals. To hide their identities, they wore robes and hoods. This group disappeared temporarily in the 1870s.

**Ku Klux Klan parade in Washington D.C.
on September 13, 1926**

About 1915, the Klan resurfaced. Interest was fueled by the growing number of immigrants entering the country. The Klan also became a powerful political force.

By the 1930s, the influence of the Klan dropped. Only local groups remained strong. For the next 30 years, the organization all but disappeared.

During the 1960s, civil rights workers attempted to force the South to accept the Civil Rights Act of 1964. There were numerous bombings, whippings, and shootings. These were carried out in secret. But many thought the acts were the work of Klansmen.

Though the organization continued some of its activities into the late 20th century, cases of Klan violence became more isolated. Its membership declined to a few thousand.

When World War I began, European immigration had almost stopped. At the same time, more factories opened. Employers needed workers. They looked to the South and found ready hands. At that time, one young African American migrant wrote "I don't Care where so long as I Go where a man is a man."

Dubois

Two million African Americans migrated to northern cities by 1930. Like the European immigrants, they moved to find freedom and work. And they sent back glowing reports. In the North, they earned good wages. Their children went to good schools. They were treated with more respect. And they could vote.

Hurston

But Northern racism soon became a problem. Children fought racial battles in schools. White gangs attacked black people in parks. White people organized to keep African Americans out of their neighborhoods.

African Americans in the North fought back against racism. They founded the National Association for the Advancement of Colored People (NAACP). In the North, African Americans also found positions of honor and other ways to express their feelings. W. E. B. DuBois taught in universities. Zora Neale Hurston and Richard Wright wrote books. Langston Hughes wrote poetry.

Wright

Hughes

Many of Hughes's poems describe the racism he experienced. In "I Am the Darker Brother," Hughes writes about being sent to the kitchen when company came. But he says that tomorrow he'll sit at the table with company. No one will tell him to go to the kitchen because he or she will finally see how beautiful he is and be ashamed.

⊶ CLOSING THE DOOR ⊷

In 1900, the United States had 76 million people. In 1910, it had grown to 92 million. By 1920, the number was almost 106 million.

Prejudice against immigrants grew stronger after World War I. New laws limited the number of people entering the U.S.

By 1925, immigration dropped below 300,000. By 1931, fewer than 100,000 immigrants came to the United States. The nation of immigrants had closed the door.

3
chapter

LABOR AND ORGANIZING

*P*hilippe Lemay began working in the **textile** mills at the age of eight. Years later, he became a boss.

One day, inspectors came to the factory to check the ages of the workers. Lemay hid the younger workers. "There was no harm to anybody in that, and it did a lot of good," he explained after the incident. "Their parents were poor and needed every cent they could get."

In the early 20th century, everyone worked. But not everyone believed children should work. In some states, laws said that young children could not work. They had to be 14 years old to work in a factory. Other states had no child-labor laws.

Mother Jones was a union organizer. She did not want young children to work. In her autobiography, she wrote

> *I told an immense crowd of the horrors of child labor in the mills around the **anthracite** region and I showed them some of the children. I showed them Eddie Dunphy, a little fellow of twelve, whose job it was to sit all day on a high stool, handing in the right thread to another worker. Eleven hours a day he sat on the high stool with dangerous machinery all about him. All day long, winter and summer, spring and fall, for three dollars a week.*

Mother Jones

Mother Jones was born in Ireland in 1830. Her name was Mary Harris. Her father immigrated to the United States. After he earned money to pay for tickets, his family came too.

Mary Harris worked as a teacher and a dressmaker. Then she married and had four children. Her husband was an ironworker in Memphis. He belonged to a union.

A yellow fever **epidemic** swept Memphis. Her husband and children all died. So Mary Harris Jones moved to Chicago. Soon she became a union organizer. She became known as Mother Jones.

Mother Jones worked with many different unions. She traveled across the country. Sometimes she was jailed. But

President Coolidge and
Mother Jones

nothing stopped her. She spent the rest of her long life
organizing workers. Her slogan was "Pray for the dead
and fight . . . for the living."

In 1903, workers in textile factories organized a strike. A strike happens when workers walk off their jobs. They don't return to work until an agreement is made with the owners.

Some 75,000 workers in Pennsylvania walked out. They earned less than ten dollars a week. They wanted better wages. They worked for 13 hours a day and wanted shorter hours. About 10,000 of the workers were children. Most of the rest were women.

Mother Jones went to Pennsylvania. She organized the children.

Should a 12-year-old child work in a factory? Should a 12-year-old child work a 13-hour day? Pennsylvania law said children could begin work at 12. But many workers were younger than that.

In her autobiography, Mother Jones described what she saw.

Every day little children came into Union Headquarters, some with their hands off, some with the thumb missing, some with their fingers off at the knuckle. They were stooped things, round-shouldered and skinny.

Mother Jones organized a children's march. She led striking children across Pennsylvania, New Jersey, and New York. All along the way, newspapers wrote about the children. Organizers begged for a national law against child labor.

Mother Jones told crowds

Fifty years ago, there was a cry against slavery. Men gave up their lives to stop the selling of black children on the block. Today the white child is sold for two dollars a *week to the manufacturers. Fifty years ago the black babies were sold **C.O.D.** Today the white baby is sold on the **installment plan**.*

Mother Jones and the children tried to see President Roosevelt, but they did not succeed. No national law against child labor was passed.

But the strikers won some victories. They won a 52-hour work week and a pay raise. Soon after, Pennsylvania passed another law. The new law raised the working age. It said children had to be at least 14 to work in factories.

⋙ ORGANIZING UNIONS ⋘

Throughout the 19th century, workers had fought for better pay. They organized unions. They tried to get shorter workdays. Sometimes they succeeded. More often, the powerful employers defeated the union.

Sometimes workers went on strike. Employers fired them. New workers were easily hired to take the jobs. The population had more than doubled between the Civil War and 1900. So there were plenty of workers.

Workers did not give up. They kept on organizing unions. Women in textile factories formed the International Ladies Garment Workers Union. Men in mines began the United Mine Workers. Railroad workers, steelworkers, hatmakers, and longshoremen organized.

Unions won more and more battles. Some won shorter hours. Others won better pay. Still others won safer working conditions.

The American Federation of Labor (AFL) brought many unions together. By 1904, over 1.7 million workers belonged to the AFL.

The AFL pushed for an eight-hour day for workers. Its member unions worked for higher pay. They also asked for safer, healthier workplaces.

Samuel Gompers

Samuel Gompers helped organize the American Federation of Labor. The AFL became the leading organization in the labor movement. Gompers was its first president and served for 37 years.

Gompers

Gompers was born in London, England. As a boy of ten, he was **apprenticed** to a shoemaker. He didn't like the work. So he managed to change to cigar making. His family moved from England to America when Gompers was 13.

Gompers worked as a cigar maker in New York. His fellow workers saw him as a leader. He helped to organize the cigar-makers union. Then he helped get unions working together in the AFL.

In 1911, the Triangle Shirtwaist Company employed hundreds of workers. The factory was on the top floors of a ten-story building in New York.

On the afternoon of March 25, 1911, a fire broke out. Firefighters rushed to the factory. Their ladders could not reach the top floors.

Factory doors were locked. Workers could not get out.

Workers began to leap from the windows. About 150 workers died. Some were trapped in the blaze. Others died as they plunged to the ground.

A crowd gathers on the street during the fire. The Triangle Shirtwaist Company is in the building on the left.

New York had safety laws before the Triangle fire. Those laws said doors must open outward. Triangle's doors opened inward. The laws said exit doors could not be locked. Triangle's doors were locked because the company said it did not want workers leaving during work hours. The laws were on the books, but what good were they? They had not been enforced.

Family members arrive to identify the bodies of victims of the fire.

GOVERNMENT: WHOSE SIDE IS IT ON?

The government often became involved in labor disputes. In New York, legislators passed a maximum-hours law. This law limited the hours that workers could be ordered to work in a week. Bosses challenged the law. And the U.S. Supreme Court declared the law unconstitutional.

Another law protected union members. It said a person could not be fired just for being a union member. Again, bosses challenged the law. And once again, the Supreme Court said the law was unconstitutional.

During strikes, courts often helped the employers rather than the workers. An injunction is an order to do what the court says or go to jail. Many courts issued these orders against strikers. Then police could arrest and jail the strike's leaders.

Police arrested strikers on many charges. If strikers demonstrated, they were said to have "disturbed the peace." Strike leaders might have "incited riots." Marchers might have "trespassed on company property."

Sometimes city police acted. Sometimes the companies hired private police. Some officers beat strikers instead of arresting them.

Sometimes the government tried to help. In 1902, coal miners struck in Pennsylvania. After five months, the government stepped in. President Roosevelt pressured both sides. The union and the company accepted **mediation**. The federal mediators settled the strike.

Death in Colorado

In 1913, coal miners struck in Ludlow, Colorado. They demanded better pay and safety in the mines. One of the strike leaders was murdered. Miners protested his murder.

The miners lived in shacks owned by the company. When they went on strike, the company **evicted** them. So the United Mine Workers union provided tents for the miners and their families.

The governor sent in the **National Guard**. The National Guard beat miners and arrested them. Still the miners continued their strike. They stayed in their tents through the cold winter.

On April 20, 1914, the National Guard attacked. They fired machine guns at the tent city. Some strikers fired back. Women and children dug pits in the tents. They crouched in the pits, hiding from the bullets. Finally, the National Guard set fire to the tents.

Thirteen people were killed by gunfire. Eleven children and two women burned to death in the tents.

Surviving miners took to the hills. They carried all the weapons they could find. President Woodrow Wilson finally sent in the army to restore order.

Sticking to the Union

The workers' deaths in New York and Colorado brought change. Across the nation, their deaths were mourned. Efforts to organize workers continued with new interest.

Gradually, unions gained more power. Politicians listened to workers. Some states passed laws for safe workplaces. Others limited the hours of work.

The laws changed slowly. The federal government finally recognized workers' rights. One law protected railroad workers. Another protected federal employees. Sailors gained legal protection. So did children.

In 1913, the government established the Department of Labor.

Unions won many victories. The road ahead was still hard. The first national minimum wage law would not come until 1938. That law would set a minimum wage of 25 cents an hour.

Union Organizations

The Knights of Labor began in 1869. It started as a secret society to protect workers. It was open to shopkeepers and farmers as well as other workers.

The AFL started in 1886. The AFL included mostly craft unions or more skilled workers. The AFL did not want industrial workers. Some industrial workers worked on assembly lines. Many were unskilled laborers.

In 1905, the International Workers of the World (IWW) appeared. This union was also known as the Wobblies. The IWW wanted all workers in one big union. They also wanted a revolution.

In 1935, industrial unions began to split off from the AFL. They formed the Congress of Industrial Organizations in 1938. In 1955, the two union federations joined. They became the AFL-CIO.

---

chapter

TECHNOLOGY AND CULTURE

The 20th century changed U.S. culture. In the previous century, only rich people followed fashion. Now, fashion affected everyone. Skirts and hair grew shorter. A few women dared to wear trousers. Many tried lipstick and makeup for the first time.

Other changes came from technology. Assembly lines changed the nature of work. Electric lights replaced candles and gaslights. Automobiles meant greater mobility. Technology transformed the country.

Henry Ford in the driver's seat of his Model T Ford

Henry Ford did not invent automobiles, the assembly line, or mass production. What he did was to combine all three. He put America into automobiles.

In 1907, Ford announced

> *I will build a motor car for the great multitude. It will be large enough for the family but small enough for the individual to run and care for. . . . But it will be so low in price that no man making a good salary will be unable to own one . . .*

The key to success was his Model T. The Model T was also called the Tin Lizzie. The Tin Lizzie was simple to make. It was easy to drive. And it came in just one color—black.

Ford made the same car from 1908 to 1927. In 1909, he sold 12,000 cars. Each 1909 Model T cost $950.

In 1917, Ford sold almost 800,000 cars. As he sold more cars, the price dropped. By 1928, the cost of each car was down to $290.

Automobiles changed daily life. First, they cleaned up city streets. As cars took the place of horses, manure disappeared. That meant better-smelling, less germ-ridden streets.

With more cars came more highways. People wanted to travel farther. Eventually, cars would lead to suburbs. People would move out of city apartments. They would leave crowded streets behind. They would build single-family homes with green spaces for children to play. Then they would get in their cars and drive to work.

⊷═◉ KEEPING WORKERS ◉═⊶

In 1913, Ford's Detroit factories provided 13,600 jobs. Unskilled workers earned less than two dollars a day. Assembly line work was hard and boring. So workers came and went. In 1913, about 50,400 people quit or were fired from Ford's Detroit factories. That's more than a 350 percent turnover.

Hiring and training new workers was **inefficient**. Henry Ford wanted **efficiency**. Besides, angry or unhappy workers could be dangerous. An angry worker could **sabotage** a whole assembly line.

Sabotage

Sabotage was a word that came from factory life. In Belgium and northern France, workers wore wooden shoes. The shoes were called *sabots*. Throwing a wooden shoe into machinery could wreck the machinery. This was called *sabotage*.

Ford also worried about unions. Unhappy workers were more likely to join unions. The IWW tried to organize autoworkers. How could Ford keep his employees from joining? How could he prevent strikes or sabotage?

His solution was simple but shocking. In 1914, Ford raised wages. He announced that workers who met his standards would be paid five dollars a day. For this wage, Ford required good behavior on and off the job. For example, workers could not use tobacco or alcohol.

Five dollars a day! No one paid that much for unskilled labor. Workers lined up to get Ford jobs. Those lucky enough to land a job, kept it. By 1915, annual turnover dropped to 16 percent.

Satisfied workers meant higher profits. Better-paid workers gave Ford something more. Now the men who made cars could afford to buy cars. Ford's own workers became a new market for his products.

⤙ ELECTRIFYING THE NATION ⤚

Thomas Edison invented the electric light in 1879. By 1903, more than a thousand electric power stations lit up the country.

Electricity powered factories as well as lights.

After World War I, new appliances reached homes. Electric sewing machines speeded up sewing. Vacuum cleaners took the place of beating rugs. Electric washing machines made laundry easier. Electric stoves, toasters, and mixers changed kitchens.

Mass production of food changed the way people ate. After 1900, canned foods appeared in stores. Some homes even had refrigerators.

In 1915, advertisements promised laborsaving days for homemakers. Van Camp ads said its pork and beans would save "100 hours yearly."

The new appliances changed family life. In 1900, the average family spent 44 hours each week preparing meals and washing dishes. By 1925, they needed only 30 hours.

In 1900, the average family spent seven hours a week doing laundry. By 1925, that time was down to five hours.

Electric power also changed manufacturing. Use of electric power in manufacturing doubled between 1909 and 1914. And its use continued to grow.

FROM PIANOS IN THE PARLOR TO PHONOGRAPH

Before the phonograph, there was sheet music. Many people played pianos. They learned popular songs and sang them with friends. Songs with simple melodies and lots of **choruses** were popular.

Ragtime was a new kind of music that appeared in the early 1900s. Ragtime started as African American music. Then it became widely popular.

Scott Joplin was called the King of Ragtime. He was African American. He had a classical music education. But the music he wrote was ragtime. His "Maple Leaf Rag" sold more than a million copies of sheet music.

White musicians wrote ragtime too. Irving Berlin, a Russian American composer, wrote "Alexander's Ragtime Band."

Ragtime moved into the big time. People listened to orchestras play ragtime and danced to it at dance halls and restaurants. They learned to dance the turkey trot, the fox-trot, and the tango.

Phonographs allowed people to buy recordings. As phonographs became popular, more musicians recorded music. People didn't need to buy sheet music and make music themselves.

Now jazz and blues appeared on the scene. With them, came more African American musicians.

Classical musicians also made recordings for phonographs. Enrico Caruso, an opera singer, made many records.

Caruso, second from the left

From 1910 to 1929, more than 900,000 African Americans left the South. They came north during World War I and found work in factories. After the war, many came north looking for a life with more freedom. They settled in Chicago, Detroit, and New York.

One man wrote a letter to family still in the South.

I should have been here 20 years ago. I [am] just [beginning] to feel like a man. It's a great deal of pleasure in knowing that you have got some privilege. My children are going to the same school with the whites and I don't have to [h]umble to no one. I have registered — Will vote the next election and there isn[']t any "yes sir" and "no sir" — it's all yes and no and Sam and Bill.

In New York, black immigrants settled in Harlem. Some came from the South. Others came from the West Indies.

Cullen

Writers, actors, and musicians lived in Harlem. They made this part of the city exciting. Harlem became a center for culture.

Louis Armstrong trumpeted jazz into the musical mainstream. Langston Hughes and Countee Cullen wrote poetry.

Zora Neale Hurston wrote stories and plays. As an African American writer, she wanted to be in New York. Hurston once wrote that she could set her hat "at a certain angle and saunter down Seventh Avenue, Harlem City, feeling as snooty as the lions in front of the Forty-second Street Library."

White people flocked to Harlem to hear these exciting new voices. Black and white New Yorkers met in clubs and cafes. For some whites, "Negroes" were suddenly fashionable.

MAKING WAVES WITH RADIO AND MOVIES

Before 1920, radio was used to communicate with ships at sea. Then big business decided to make it something more. General Electric, RCA, and AT&T joined forces. Together, they decided how to manufacture and market radios. The first commercial broadcast was in Pittsburgh on November 2, 1920. Radio station KDKA announced the election results.

Then radio took off. In 1920, one radio was sold for every 500 homes.

40

By 1926, one radio was sold for every six homes. Radios still broadcast news, but music was center stage.

By 1925, music took up more than 70 percent of radio time. Now everyone with a radio could listen to jazz bands and big bands play popular music.

Sports and politics took the microphone too. In 1926, more than 50 million people listened to a boxing match between Jack Dempsey and Gene Tunney.

Nickelodeons sold moving pictures across the country. People paid a nickel to see a feature film and one or two short films. The movies were silent. The actors' words flashed across the screen. Piano players in the theater made music to fit the mood. In 1910, at least 5,000 nickelodeons were in the United States.

⟬ POPULAR CULTURE ⟭

Once, the rich owned culture. Only the rich could attend plays and concerts. Only they had the leisure time to read books. In the 20th century, all that changed.

No longer did a family need a piano to play the latest music. Now they could play a record on a phonograph. The radio brought national news to millions at the same time.

Moving pictures were available across the country.

Culture now belonged to the people.

⟬ PROHIBITION ⟭

The new forms of culture did not please everyone. Many people objected. They thought jazz and movies encouraged sin. These people preached old-fashioned moral values. They spoke out against dancing and drinking.

Nation, with hatchet and Bible

Most of all, many were against drinking. Carrie Nation was a **militant** opponent of alcohol. She held prayer meetings in saloons to close them. She also attacked saloons and smashed bottles, windows, and tables.

The **temperance** movement worked to make alcohol illegal. Most temperance activists were less **flamboyant** than Carrie Nation. But their work succeeded.

In 1920, the Eighteenth Amendment to the U.S. Constitution banned the manufacture, transportation, or sale of alcohol. Prohibition had begun.

Many people still wanted to drink. Illegal sale of alcohol boomed. **Bootleggers** sold liquor to individuals. **Speakeasies** were clubs that sold drinks at high prices. These clubs were hidden behind false doors. They often required a password to enter. All were illegal. During Prohibition, breaking the law became fashionable.

From the earliest days of U.S. history, women sought a voice in government. John Adams had helped write the constitution. Later, he became the second president of the United States. While he was working on the constitution, his wife wrote to him. "Do not forget the ladies," Abigail Adams pleaded. Neither her husband nor the other men listened.

John Adams

During the 19th century, many women worked for justice. They worked to abolish slavery. They worked to win the vote for themselves. But as the 20th century began, women still had not won suffrage.

Ragtime Suffragette

The "Ragtime Suffragette" was written by Harry Williams and Nat D. Thayer. The song used music to comment on women's struggle for the vote.

What's that noise upon the avenue?

What's that crowd a-doin' 'round there too?

What's the meaning of that awful crash?

Has a taxicab got in a smash?

Johnny, Johnny run and get your gun.

Get in quick or you'll be dead, my son.

It would make Napoleon quake

And shake his head with fear.

Oh dear, oh dear, just look, look, look who's here;

That ragtime suffragette,
She's no household pet,
Raggin' with bombshells and raggin' with bricks,
Raggin' and naggin' with politics,
That ragtime suffragette,
Ragtime suffragette,
For Lordy, while her husband's wait home to dine,
She's just rag-gin' up and down the line.
A-shoutin' votes, votes, votes for women,
She's a ragtime suffragette.

Now the struggle took two parallel paths. Carrie Chapman Catt led the National Association for Women's Suffrage (NAWS). NAWS worked for legal changes, state by state. In many states, women won the right to vote in state elections. But they still could not vote in national elections.

Women's suffrage march

Other women believed in radical action. Led by Alice Paul, they formed the Congressional Union. They pressured presidents and Congress. They marched and demonstrated. Sometimes they went to jail.

The combined efforts of suffragists succeeded. In 1920, the Nineteenth Amendment to the U.S. Constitution gave women the right to vote.

Catt

44

chapter

THE BIG STICK

☞ CLOSE TO HOME ☜

"Speak softly and carry a big stick," advised President Theodore Roosevelt. He kept the "big stick" in plain view. Sometimes he used it.

The big stick was military force. The United States often used military force in Latin America.

The United States wanted to build a canal to connect the Atlantic and Pacific oceans. It would run through Colombia.

The United States demanded control of the canal for 100 years. Soldiers in bases near the canal would control the land nearby. In exchange, the U.S. would pay $10 million. It would also pay $250,000 a year in rent. Colombia refused the deal.

Roosevelt was furious. He thought about invading Colombia. Instead, he watched a revolution in one of Colombia's provinces. The province of Panama had declared its independence.

The United States agreed to protect that independence. So Panama agreed to U.S. terms for the canal.

Now the United States could build its new canal. U.S. troops would remain in Panama for almost a century.

Panama Canal wrecking crew

Panama Canal

In the mid-1800s, people wanted a faster way of getting from Europe to western North and South America. In 1881, the French began a project in Panama. They planned to dig a canal across the tiny country and connect the Atlantic and Pacific Oceans.

After the French project failed, the Americans took over in 1904. The canal was completed in 1914. It saved about 18,000 miles of sea travel between New York City and San Francisco. That trip took five to six months going around the southern tip of South America. Now the trip, using the canal, took five to six weeks.

The United States controlled the canal and

Building of the Panama Canal

surrounding land for almost a century. On December 31, 1999, control of the canal was formally turned over to Panama. The United States still maintains a military base in the Canal Zone.

Roosevelt warned Europe to stay out of Latin America. Instead, the United States would police Latin America. The big stick went to work. Roosevelt—and presidents after him—repeatedly invaded Latin American countries. Sometimes they overthrew governments. Sometimes they just protected U.S. and European investments.

⟫ AND FAR AWAY ⟪

The United States tried to stay out of European politics. Then came the Great War.

While it was happening, people called this war the Great War. After the Second World War, people called it World War I.

The Great War grew out of old **rivalries**. On one side stood the Allies—Britain, France, and Russia. On the other was Germany and Austria-Hungary.

The spark that lit the fire was struck in Sarajevo. It came on June 28, 1914. A Bosnian student assassinated an Austrian archduke. Within days, the war was on. Before it ended, the war would involve 27 countries on four continents.

The United States wanted to stay out of the war. President Wilson said the U.S. would remain **neutral**. After all, U.S. citizens came from all of the warring countries. Though Wilson favored Britain and France, he did not want the United States divided.

⇢═ CLOSER TO WAR ═⇠

Britain controlled the seas. That meant that Britain controlled trade routes. U.S. manufacturers were happy to trade with Britain. U.S. businesses grew rich selling arms and supplies.

In 1914, the United States sold about $825 million in goods to the Allies. By 1916, the amount increased to $3.2 billion. U.S. industry boomed. Weapon sales made up more than a third of the sales.

In 1916, Wilson campaigned for reelection. One of his slogans was, "He kept us out of war." Wilson won a second term. Then he led the country into war.

U.S. businesses made money shipping products to the Allies. So the U.S. wanted the Allies to win the war. But the Allies were not doing well. They needed the U.S. to join the war effort.

German submarines were sinking Allied ships. They even sank a few U.S. ships. U.S. businesses lost money with each sinking ship. So now the U.S. businesses were ready for war.

⇢═ OPPOSITION AT HOME ═⇠

Many Americans opposed the war. Some were **isolationists**. Some were **pacifists**. Some were socialists.

Isolationists did not want the United States involved in European affairs. They wanted to keep the United States out of foreign politics and especially out of foreign wars.

Pacifists did not believe in war at all. They wanted peaceful solutions to problems. They believed killing was wrong. They believed war did not solve anything.

Some African Americans opposed the war. Why should their young men fight for a country that did not protect them at home? Why should they fight to keep a world safe for segregation?

In Oklahoma, opponents of the war staged a rebellion. Farmers, African Americans, and Native Americans joined together. They cut pipelines and burned bridges.

In 1917, the rebels planned to march on Washington D.C. They said they would pick "green corn" along the way and carry it all the way to Washington. The corn would ripen in the sun. People called this the Green Corn Rebellion.

The rebels never reached Washington. Instead, 450 people ended up in prison.

Socialists also opposed the war. They said the fighting was between **capitalists**. It was not a war for workers' freedom. It was a war for greater profits for employers. It was a war between businesses fighting over how to divide the profits.

Eugene Debs, a Socialist leader, once told a crowd

Wars throughout history have always been waged for conquest and plunder . . . And that is war in a nutshell. The master class has always declared the wars; the subject class has always fought the battles . . .

⇒ INTO THE WAR ⇐

In 1917, Wilson asked congress to enter the war. Congress agreed. Quickly, congress passed a **draft** bill. Patriotic slogans sprang up. This war would "make the world safe for democracy." It would be "the war to end all wars."

Most Americans quickly came to support the war. They bought war bonds. They sang **patriotic** songs. They watched patriotic movies.

Before the war ended, about 10 million soldiers died. Some 130,000 of that number were U.S. soldiers. Another 20 million people died of hunger and disease because of the war.

⇒ ON THE HOME FRONT ⇐

The United States was changed by war. Now a piano factory made airplane wings. A clothing factory made uniforms. Another made signal flags. Weapons, gas masks, medical supplies—all were made for the war effort.

Factories increased production. They desperately needed workers. At the time, more than six million men had been drafted.

As "Help Wanted" signs went up, barriers came down. Some factories hired African Americans for the first time. Others hired women for the first time. The war made work for all.

Food, too, was needed for the war effort. Farmers were urged to produce all they could. Prices for farm products rose.

Women working in ammunition factory

Europe and the army needed food. People at home were encouraged to cut back. They kept "wheatless" days and "meatless" days. On those days, they didn't eat products made from wheat or meat.

⊶ THE WAR AGAINST DEMOCRACY ⊷

President Wilson preached that the war would "make the world safe for democracy." On the home front, it looked more like the war against democracy.

Free speech was an early victim of the war. Congress passed laws saying no one could speak against the war. People who spoke against the war or the draft were arrested.

Socialists, **anarchists**, and labor unionists were special targets. Already unpopular, they were jailed by the hundreds.

And then the war ended. The Allies won. But would life ever return to normal?

AMERICA IN THE WORLD

After the Great War, U.S. soldiers came home. Their return seemed symbolic. Most Americans wanted to stay home. Their songs reflected this feeling. They sang of "Rose of Washington Square." They celebrated "Chicago—That Toddlin' Town." They danced on "The Sidewalks of New York." They rejoiced to be "Back in Your Own Backyard."

LEAGUE OF NATIONS

President Wilson was an **idealist**. He believed the world was now "safe for democracy." He wanted to keep it that way. So did many other world leaders.

These leaders proposed a League of Nations. The League would include all the countries of the world. It would keep the hard-won peace.

Congress did not like the idea. It refused to allow the United States to be part of the League of Nations.

Americans wanted to forget Europe and its troubles. They never wanted another European war. When Congress voted down the League of Nations, the people did not object.

Wilson speaking in front of the League of Nations

THE RED SCARE

In the middle of the Great War, a revolution was taking place in Russia. The country was split. The wealthy backed the czar, who was the current leader. The poor wanted change. They were supported by the **Communists**. Words gave way to swords and bullets.

When the fighting ended, Russia had changed forever. The czar and his family were dead. The Communist party ruled.

Torn by civil war, Russia pulled out of the Great War in 1918. Without Russia as an enemy, the Germans could focus on England and France. That was when the United States entered the war.

Communism spread to the United States. Americans started two U.S. communist parties. The supporters called for a U.S. revolution. Many were arrested and jailed.

Most Americans feared communism. To them, communism was new and foreign and it meant revolution.

⇒ STRIKES AND "RACE RIOTS" ⇐

As the Great War ended, workers went on strike again. They wanted more money and shorter hours. New York harbor workers struck in January 1919. They were followed by textile workers and railroad workers. In Seattle, all the unions struck. In September, steelworkers left their jobs in protest. Even Boston's police went on strike.

In Arkansas, African American tenant farmers formed a union. They demanded better treatment by landlords.

Instead, the African Americans were attacked by whites from Mississippi and Tennessee. Before it was over, 25 African Americans were killed. Five whites died. The country called it a *race riot*.

Sixty-five African Americans were arrested. They were charged with rebellion. They were all convicted. Similar race riots took place in Chicago and Washington.

Communist, or *red*, became an easy label. Did a union demand more pay? It must be a communist plot. Did black people demand their rights? They must be communists. Did immigrants speak a different language? Maybe they were reds too.

Harding

⇒ BACK TO NORMALCY ⇐

Warren G. Harding promised "a return to normalcy." In 1920, he was elected president. The people wanted that normalcy.

chapter

A NORMAL RECESSION

I n a **recession**, there are no jobs. Farm prices fall. People go hungry. In about 1920, the United States slid into a recession.

Recessions were nothing new. Rose Wilder Lane wrote in an essay for the Federal Writers' Project about the recession of 1893.

The Federal Writers' Project was a program started by President Franklin D. Roosevelt in the 1930s. Unemployed artists, writers, musicians, actors, directors, and painters could work directly for the government. At its peak, the project employed about 6,500 men and women, paying them $20 a week. The Federal Writers produced a series of state guidebooks that offered a sampling of life in the U.S. During the late 1930s, more than 10,000 men and women from a variety of regions, occupations, and ethnic groups were interviewed. Saul Bellow, John Cheever, Ralph Ellison, and Zora Neale Hurston were some of the writers who conducted the interviews.

Roosevelt

Rose Wilder Lane wrote

> *It was a saying in the Dakotas that the Government bet a quarter section against fifteen dollars and five years' hard work that the land would starve a man out in less than five years. My father won the bet. It took seven successive years of complete crop failure, with work, weather, and sickness that wrecked his health permanently, and interest rates of 36 per cent on money borrowed to buy food, to dislodge us from that land. . . . This was during the panic of '93.*

Rose Wilder Lane was born December 5, 1886, in De Smet, Dakota Territory. De Smet is now a town in South Dakota. She was the first child of Almanzo and Laura Ingalls Wilder. Laura Ingalls Wilder was the author of the Little House books.

Recession came again in 1907. Mrs. Earl Marshall, the wife of a North Carolina farmer, remembered that time.

> *[W]e just got married. That was in 1907. . . . There was no assistance offered to struggling farmers in those days. People in all walks of life just had to fight their own battles and manage as best they could. My husband managed to find a little work here and there. . . . What little work he did manage to find brought him only 40 [cents] a day, and very often he was not fully paid when the work was done.*

In 1914, the United States was in a recession again. This time, World War I ended the recession. Europe bought food and weapons. The United States prospered.

After the war, Europeans had little money. They no longer needed weapons. They could grow their own food again. They could also import cheaper wheat from Australia.

So U.S. exports dropped dramatically. The United States sank back into a recession.

HARD TIMES ON THE FARM

During the war, many farmers borrowed money. They needed it to buy tractors. New machines helped them produce more wheat and corn. Some farmers bought more land. From 1910 to 1920, the amount of farm mortgages doubled. In 1910, farmers across the country owed $3.3 billion on mortgages. By 1920, they owed $6.7 billion.

After the war, the farm market collapsed. Prices for farm products fell. Now it cost farmers more to produce wheat than they were paid for it. They could not pay the interest on mortgages. They could not buy seed to plant.

Year	Wheat Price (per bushel)
1913 (before the war)	$0.79
1919 (just after the end of the war)	$2.16
1923	$0.93

Poverty grew like a weed in rural America. By the end of the 1920s, the average annual U.S. income was $750 per person. Average farm income was $273 per person.

⋙ LEAVING THE LAND ⋘

Machines helped make farms bigger. A farmer and a team of horses could break up 3 acres of sod a day. A tractor could plow 50 acres in a day. Cotton gins, harvesters, and mowing machines made farming more productive. Small farms were put together to make bigger farms.

But across the United States, farmers left the land. They could no longer make a living from farming.

⋙ UNEMPLOYMENT ⋘

During the recession, people lost their jobs. In 1921, unemployment rose above ten percent.

Many people were looking for work. Strikers had a tough time because there were always unemployed people to fill their jobs. The long steel strike ended in 1920. The steelworkers won nothing.

Coal miners struck for better wages. They, too, were forced back to work without a raise. Many miners worked for two dollars a day. Often, they worked less than 150 days a year.

Even "good" jobs might not be so good. Studies showed problems at Ford.

Ford speeded up assembly lines. Workers wore out. Ford often fired middle-aged workers.

Then General Motors started selling more cars. Henry Ford closed his factories, putting 60,000 workers out of work.

Henry Ford was glad to close the factories for a while. He said it did the workers good "to let them know that things are not going along too even . . ."

The Ford factories were remodeled. Now they were ready to make the new Model A. Many of the former workers came back. They had to start again as new employees. They earned the new employee salary of five dollars a day.

CHANGE IS ALL THAT STAYS THE SAME

Unions grew strong. Then bosses destroyed unions. Farms grew bigger. Then farmers went bankrupt. Contradictions filled the country. The end of the war brought change. Change scared some people. But others thought it promised an ever-brighter future.

chapter

ROARING TWENTIES

"Moonshine agents" with a smashed still

 ℛ rohibition became law in 1920. The new law made drinking illegal. Booze promptly became the focus of the twenties. More people started drinking. Everybody talked about it. Sometimes they seemed to speak a whole new language.

"Bathtub gin" could actually have been stirred up in a bathtub. Bad "moonshine" or "hooch" might have killed drinkers.

"Rum runners" smuggled booze into the country. "Moonshiners" hid **stills** in the woods. "Bootleggers" sold booze. "Speakeasies" and "gin mills" sold liquor too. And it seemed that everybody bought it.

Tex Guinah ran speakeasies in New York. Everyone had heard of Tex. She was famous—or **infamous**. Tiny padlocks dangled from her necklace. Each padlock stood for a time she had been arrested.

Flapper

Tex moved her speakeasies often. She'd find a new basement and open up. Then federal agents would find her, and she'd be forced to move again.

Famous actors drank at Tex's speakeasies. Musicians played jazz. Gangsters mingled with politicians. **Flappers** showed off their short hair and skirts. Everybody danced the Charleston. Prohibition made criminals of respectable people. It made criminals seem almost respectable.

⋯⇔ NEW WEALTH ⇔⋯

After the grimness of war and recession, people wanted to forget. They earned more money. The normal work week dropped from 60 to 48 hours. People had more time to play.

The twenties roared on.

Rich people made lots of money. They spent it too. The middle class made less money. But they wanted to spend. So they used credit. The installment plan became popular. You could buy a car for five dollars down and five dollars a month. For a radio, it was a dollar down and a dollar a week!

The twenties roared on.

Rich people bought fancy cars and jewels. They spent money on wild parties and caviar. The middle class bought Model Ts, Model As, and washing machines. The middle class bought convenient canned food. Everyone went to movies. They all bought phonographs and records.

The twenties roared on.

⟨⟩ AVOIDING POLITICS ⟨⟩

Harding

People wanted to avoid seriousness. Less than half bothered to vote for president in 1920. Warren G. Harding won the election.

Money marked his presidency. Corrupt politicians stole from the government. Harding ignored them. In 1923, he died and Calvin Coolidge became president.

Then the Teapot Dome scandal broke wide open. Teapot Dome was a hill in Wyoming. Under it lay huge oil fields. Teapot Dome and other oil fields were supposed to supply the navy. Instead, they were leased to wealthy corporations.

Private investors made millions.

The new president investigated. Politicians and businessmen went to jail. But did anyone care?

Coolidge was a Republican. In 1924, after finishing Harding's term, Coolidge ran for president.

Coolidge

During this election, a battle over the Ku Klux Klan split the Democratic party. Many southern Democrats belonged to the Klan. The Democratic convention tried to condemn the Klan. It failed. Because of the party split, none of the popular Democrats could win the nomination. Finally, the party nominated John Davis to run against Coolidge. Everyone knew he would not win.

The Progressives did not like either candidate. They were still serious about politics. They did not want to forget the poor. They did not want to ignore corruption.

Robert LaFollette was a Republican Senator from Wisconsin. He ran for president as a Progressive. He received almost five million votes. But that was not enough to win.

Once again, fewer than half the people bothered to vote. "Silent Cal" Coolidge won the election.

"Silent Cal" didn't say much. But he had a great sense of humor. One time, a society lady tried to get him to talk. She said, "I made a bet I could get more than two words out of you." President Coolidge replied, "You lose."

Many Americans still struggled to buy food and pay rent. They didn't wear new fashions. They didn't drive new cars. They washed clothes by hand. They kept food in iceboxes, not refrigerators.

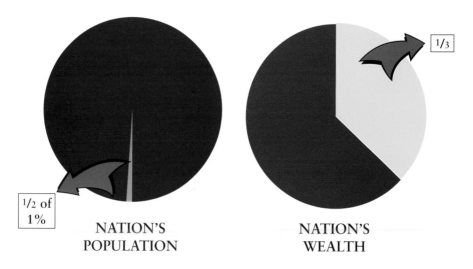

1/3

1/2 of 1%

NATION'S
POPULATION

NATION'S
WEALTH

During the 1920s, a few people were very rich. One-half of one percent of the population owned one-third of all the nation's wealth.

The nation produced great wealth. During the 1920s, productivity soared. *Productivity* means "the rate at which goods and services are produced."

Ford Motor Company is a good example. In 1920, Ford produced 25,000 cars. In 1925, Ford used almost the same machines. Ford employed about the same number of workers. But in 1925, Ford produced 31,000 cars. Productivity had increased.

From 1923 to 1929, national productivity increased by 32 percent. Wages grew by only 8 percent. Business profits rose by 62 percent. The increased productivity made companies richer. But it did not make workers richer.

Most workers were not rich at all. More than two-thirds of U.S. families earned less than $2,500 yearly. Even in 1929, this was not enough to live on. Four out of five families had no savings. Workers clung to their jobs because unemployment brought hunger and homelessness.

⇒ LOOKING AHEAD ⇐

Elections were held in 1928. This time the Democrats chose Al Smith. The Republicans chose Herbert Hoover.

Smith was the governor of New York. He was also a Catholic. The country had never elected a Catholic. To many, Catholic meant foreign.

The Ku Klux Klan campaigned against Smith. So did many others. One Methodist bishop said during the campaign

> *Governor Smith wants the Italians, the Sicilians, the Poles, and the Russian Jews. That kind has given us a stomachache. We have been unable to **assimilate** such people in our national life, so we shut the door to them. But Smith says, "Give me that kind of people." He wants the kind of dirty people you find today on the sidewalks of New York.*

Hoover

In contrast, Hoover was "all-American." During the Great War, he ran the U.S. Food Administration and directed food relief to Belgium. He had served under three presidents—Wilson, Harding, and Coolidge. He had also directed Red Cross flood relief in 1927. He was very popular.

Prejudice against Smith and Hoover's popularity combined. Hoover won by a wide margin. In his inaugural address, he said, "I have no fears for the future of our country. It is bright with hope."

That hope would be shattered in a few short months. The Great Depression was about to begin.

Sources

Books

Cashman, Sean Dennis. *America Ascendant: From Theodore Roosevelt to FDR in the Century of American Power, 1901–1945*, New York University Press, New York, NY, 1998.

Coan, Peter Morton. *Ellis Island Interviews: In Their Own Words*, Checkmark Books, New York, NY, 1997.

Davis, Kenneth C. *Don't Know Much About History: Everything You Need to Know About American History but Never Learned*, Avon Books, New York, NY, 1990, 1995.

Jones, Mary Harris. *The Autobiography of Mother Jones*, Charles Kerr, New York, NY, 1925.

McElvaine, Robert S. *The Great Depression*, Random House, New York, NY, 1984, 1995.

Takaki, Ronald. *A Different Mirror: A History of Multicultural America*, Little, Brown, Boston, MA, 1994.

Takaki, Ronald. *A Larger Memory: A History of Our Diversity with Voices*, Little, Brown, Boston, MA, 1998.

Watkins, T. H. *The Hungry Years: A Narrative History of the Great Depression in America*, Henry Holt, New York, NY, 1999.

Zinn, Howard. *A People's History of the United States: 1492–Present*, HarperPerennial, New York, NY, 1995.

Court Cases

Lochner v. New York, 1905
U.S. v. Adair, 1908

Glossary

anarchist	one who is against any form of government control or authority
anthracite	relating to hard, shiny coal
apprentice	to learn a trade or skill from someone in the field
assassinate	to kill
assimilate	to absorb
bootlegger	one who makes or distributes something illegally
bully	one who is always cruel to others who are weaker
capitalist	one who profits from money invested in a business
cavalry	relating to soldiers who ride horses
chorus	part of a song that is repeated at intervals
C.O.D.	cash on delivery
communist	one who believes in a government that owns all business and industry
corruption	act of using improper or unlawful means, such as bribery
critic	one who judges
diphtheria	severe contagious disease caused by bacteria that affect the heart and nervous system
dominate	to rule or control
draft	relating to the act of selecting an individual for military service
efficiency	best way of producing the desired result
epidemic	outbreak and rapid spread of a disease
evict	to force out
flamboyant	having colorful or elaborate behavior
flapper	young woman who disliked proper dress and behavior

icebox	cabinet that held a block of ice to keep food cold
idealist	one who sets and lives by standards for excellence
immigration	act of entering one country from another
inefficient	not producing the desired or intended result
infamous	having a bad reputation
influenza	contagious disease, caused by a virus, that causes aches, fever, and respiratory problems
installment plan	way of buying something by paying a small amount immediately and then making a series of payments weekly, monthly, or at specified times
invalid	not legally based
isolationist	one who believes that government should not have political or economic relations with other governments
lynching	hanging
mediation	act of helping two opposing parties reach an agreement
migrant	having ability to move from one place to another
militant	relating to one who is combative and aggressive
mortgage	loan on property that requires regular payments with interest
National Guard	state military unit funded equally by the federal and state governments
neutral	not taking sides in a dispute or war
nickelodeon	early movie theater where tickets cost a nickel
pacifist	one who is opposed to war or violence
patriotic	showing love and support for one's country
prejudice	preconceived judgment or opinion

racism	belief that one race is superior to all others
recession	period when public spending drops
repeal	to set aside or cancel
reservation	public land that has been set aside. Native Americans were forced to live on this land.
rivalry	act of trying to be better than another
sabotage	destruction of an employer's property
scarlet fever	contagious disease that causes a rash and a red and sore nose, throat, and mouth
scrimp	to spend only what is necessary in order to save as much money as possible
segregate	to separate
sharecropper	farmer who is provided with credit for seed, tools, living quarters, and food. The farmer works the land and receives an agreed share of the value of the crop minus charges.
socialist	relating to one who believes that the production and distribution of goods should be controlled by the government. The distribution of goods and pay depends on work done.
speakeasy	place where alcohol was sold illegally
still	equipment used to make alcohol
suffrage	right to vote
temperance	relating to the act of not using alcohol
tenant	one who rents property
tenement	apartment house in a city that meets minimum standards of sanitation, safety, and comfort
textile	relating to woven cloth
trust	combination of businesses that reduces competition
union	group of workers who join together and work for better conditions

Index

McKinley, William, 6
migrants, 18–19, 21
music
    blues, 38
    classical, 38
    jazz, 38, 39, 61
    ragtime, 38
Nation, Carrie, 42
National Association for the
    Advancement of Colored People
    (NAACP), 21
National Association for Women's
    Suffrage (NAWS), 44
Nineteenth Amendment, 44
pacifists, 48–49
Panama, 45–46, 47
Panama Canal, 45–47
Paul, Alice, 44
Phillipines, 4, 5
political parties
    Bull Moose Progressive, 8
    Democrat, 7, 8, 63, 65
    Progressive, 7, 8, 9, 63, 65
    Republican, 7, 8, 63, 65
    Socialist, 9, 49
Prohibition, 10, 11, 41–42, 60–61
Puerto Rico, 5
race riots, 54
recession, 55–59
Roaring Twenties, 60–66
Roosevelt, Franklin D., 55
Roosevelt, Theodore (Teddy), 6–7,
    8, 9, 27, 30, 45, 47
Russian Revolution, 53
Smith, Al, 65, 66

Spain, 4–5
Spanish-American War, 4, 7
Taft, William Howard, 8, 9
Teapot Dome Scandal, 62
Triangle Shirtwaist Company, 29
unions, 9, 10, 24, 26, 27–28, 30–32,
    36, 44, 54, 59
United Mine Workers, 27, 31
U.S.S. *Maine*, 4
Wilson, Woodrow, 8–9, 31, 48, 50,
    51, 52, 53
women's rights, 9, 10, 43–44
World War I (the Great War), 22,
    37, 39, 47–51, 53
Wright, Richard, 21